Roadmap Toward Destiny

Teen Handbook

Lawrence Trimble

STRONG
PUBLISHING
House

Bringing the strength of your words to reality

ISBN-13:
978-0615839042 (Strong Publishing House)
ISBN-10:
0615839045

Unless otherwise indicated, all Scripture quotations are taken from the Holy Bible, New Living Translation, copyright © 1996, 2004, 2007 by Tyndale House Foundation. Used by permission of Tyndale House Publishers, Inc., Carol Stream, Illinois 60188. All rights reserved.

Cover quotation: Tony Robbins. (n.d.). BrainyQuote.com. Retrieved June 22, 2013, from BrainyQuote.com Web site:
http://www.brainyquote.com/quotes/quotes/t/tonyrobbin147787.html
Read more at
http://www.brainyquote.com/citation/quotes/quotes/t/tonyrobbin147787.html #dIRA9LF8APMCSbJO.99

Published by **Strong Publishing House**
Inquiries: strongpublishinghouse@gmail.com
strongpublishinghouse.weebly.com

DEDICATION

To every young person who desires to walk out their God-given
purpose in the earth. God bless you and keep you!

~Lawrence

CONTENTS

1
FINDING PURPOSE IN GOD'S PLAN

From the beginning of time God has set aside a purpose for his children to live in. Before you were formed in the womb of your parents, there was a plan made for your life. As teens it is important to grasp and understand you were not created to just exist. The life of every youth should have meaning. Living without meaning will result in a meaningless life. There is a God-ordained and God-destined purpose for you while walking this earth, and it includes living as a representative of God.

Finding yourself in God's purpose

Creating Meaning for life

Having a life with meaning is important to God. Here are some questions you can ask yourself to develop purpose for your life, and live a life full of meaning.

1. What am I good at doing?

2. What are some things that I have a strong desire to do?

3. Are there some ways I can volunteer with other organizations?

4. Are there certain types of people I enjoy being around? Are there those I do not enjoy being around?

After answering these questions have an adult go over with you to find ways to enhance what you are good at.

As you understand God's plan for your life the next step is to begin to develop the purpose He has for you. Age is not a factor to God in order to walk in His purpose for your life. Jeremiah, the prophet, thought his age would be an obstacle stopping him from walking in the purpose of God. He questions God's calling him. "O Sovereign Lord", I said, "I can't speak for you!" "I'm too young!" Jeremiah 1:6 Never remove the purpose God has for you from your life based on your age. God can call the young and the old for the purpose He has in the earth. Just as Jeremiah questioned God, there will be times in your life when you question God as well, but don't let the questions stop you in the quest to fulfill God's purpose.

Once we remove fear from our lives, we will begin to walk forward in doing the work of God. Purpose is

8

What is the goal I desire to achieve in my life? -

_____

_____

_____

_____

_____

_____

_____

Will my age become a factor in stopping me achieve my goal?

_____

_____

_____

_____

_____

_____

having an end, aim, or goal to accomplish something; having an overall reason in the beginning, or during the process. When moving forward there are two things one should understand in relationship to your purpose.

1. Everything you step forward to do is for the end goal to come to past.

2. Always keep the ending goal in mind. Maintaining focus

The age obstacle cannot hinder a person with purpose because their desire is to please God. When a person's desire is to please God, they are motivated to do all God says and accomplish his work in the earth.

Don't say, "I'm too young, for you must go wherever I send you and say whatever I tell you. ~Jeremiah 1:7

God's purpose will always help in keeping you going in the correct direction. It is like the GPS system for our life. There are times when an extra boost of information is needed to get to the correct destination. When someone is travelling in a city they don't know, it is important they use a guide to prevent wandering and getting lost. God's word is the same way. In His word we find what our purpose should be, based on what His word says. During times of uncertainty it is necessary we call upon God for direction. Uncertain times are the times we should seek to get close to God through prayer, so the correct direction can be given.

Learning to pray

When we pray we can use the Lord's Prayer Matthew 6:6-13 as the example for our personal prayer time.

Make sure to have these parts:

1. Praise to God, giving reverence to him
2. Repentance for sin
3. Petition for needs of self and others
4. Direction away from sin and evil
5. Thanksgiving believing your prayers will be answered

Prayer is needed communication with God. Develop a plan to pray daily, beginning your day asking God for clear direction toward your purpose.

Prayer develops a connection with God and gives an understanding of the desire He has for your life. Without this connection you will never be able to understand what His will is. Have you ever been in a place and needed to make a very important phone call, but could not because of a lack of signal? You tried over and over again in different parts of the building, but could not gain enough signal strength to make the call? This is metaphorically how our life is without prayer. Prayer gives the signal strength we need connecting us to God, positioning us to make the correct decisions for our life.

Connecting with the overall purpose of God

The foundational piece of knowledge all Christians should have is knowing what the overall purpose God has for their life is. We all have individual lives and goals we wish to obtain. But in achieving our life plan, it is important to know God's overall plan.

But you are not like that, for you are a chosen people. You are royal priests, a holy nation, God's very own possession. As a result, you can show others the goodness of God, for he called you out of darkness into his wonderful light. ~1 Peter 2:9

There are two things we see here: 1. You are God's very own possession and 2. You show others the goodness of God. Within every individual goal we, there needs to be a reminder that we are God's people, and we show the goodness of God through our life.

No matter what educational or career path we choose when God is first, all other things will fall into the correct location for us to fulfill our purpose. Seek the Kingdom of God above all else, and live righteously, and he will give you everything you need ~Matthew 6:33. You have been chosen to be exclusive and make a lasting impact in the lives of those you come in contact with.

Seeking the Kingdom of God

1. What are ways I can seek God's Kingdom on a daily basis?

_____

_____

_____

2. How can I connect others to God through my serving them?

_____

_____

_____

God's plan for all to be saved

Regardless of the career, sport, talent, ability, or academic knowledge a person chooses, the overall plan of God is for the person to be saved. Salvation is

Receiving Salvation

-Salvation- (Soteria) means to saved or delivered from a situation.

-Jesus came so all men can receive salvation which comes from God. "For God loved the world so much that he gave his one and only Son, so that everyone who believes in him will not perish but have eternal live"
~John 3:16
"I am the way, the truth, and the life. No one can come to the Father except through me"
~John 14:6

How can I be saved?
1. Recognize need for salvation as a sinner.
~Romans 3:23- For everyone has sinned.
~Romans 6:23- For the wages of sin is death.

2. Confess Christ as Lord and Savior
~Romans 10:9- If you confess with your mouth that Jesus is Lord.

3. Live according to God's word in love.
~John 15:10- When you obey my commandments, you remain in my love.

granted to all those who accept Christ as Lord and Savior. Salvation gives access to heaven, by God's grace, as well as the ability to live as God desires. It is the choice of the individual to accept Christ as Savior. God grants a person free will to make the choice, but any rejection of God does not remove His desire for all to be saved. We were created in His image(look like) and likeness(act like), therefore God wants us to reign with Him.

When seeking God's kingdom it is important to make sure your spirit is in right standing with God. To be sure, this comes with obedience to His word. Our actions following salvation show if we have received Him or not. A person's actions show who they are connected to. If you are part of a family, certain characteristics and actions connect you all together. From annual family gatherings, accent of voice, to ways of dealing with society, all allow others to know what family you come from. It is the same in God's kingdom. Our actions show people we have accepted Him and dedicated our lives to live for Him only.

Personal Connection

1. List activities that will help you find your purpose.

_____

_____

_____

2. What does the Kingdom of God mean to me? How do I see myself in it?

_____

_____

_____

3. What can I do daily to help me look and respond like a child of God?

_____

_____

_____

2
MAKING RIGHT DECISIONS IN TOUGH SITUATIONS

Many times in life we are faced with different situations and "choices" have to be made. Making choices is not necessarily good or bad, but the result of the choice made will have positive or negative consequences. In order to fulfill God's purpose, it is necessary to pay close attention to the choices you make. As situations come, you should have concern about how the particular choice will affect your righteous pathway. Asking yourself this question will assist: Does this help me move closer to God's purpose? or Does it slow me down from moving in

God's purpose? These two questions help guide you in making the correct decisions for your life.

Plan of Satan

Satan's job is to present opportunities for you to get off track from where God wants to take you. The best way he does this is by his presentation of sin. Have you noticed some television shows, commercials, or popular songs of something good for you you. What is here is to present *The decisions I make will have a positive or negative consequence. I have to be sure to choose wisely.* have the tone not being but good to being done sin as harmless without recognizing the reality of the spiritual harm being done. By using this cunning (deceitful, tricky) practice he gains an advantage, attempting to make people fall for his deception. Satan will always attempt to deceive people who want to walk in the pathway of God's purpose, because his purpose is to have people continue in sin like the angels in heaven (Revelations 12:3-9).

Destroying Devices of Satan

What is sin?

_____
_____
_____
_____
_____
_____
_____

What does God call Satan and what is his job?
1 Peter 5:8

_____
_____
_____
_____
_____
_____

How should we conduct ourselves to be a person God is pleased with?
2 Timothy 2:21-22

_____
_____
_____
_____
_____
_____

Power of influence

The power of influence has positive and negative effects on all age groups. Many become great and not so great leaders because of this theory. We know Satan was able to use this theory in the heavens with one-third of the angelic hosts. Jesus was able to use this theory with 12 disciples who began the discipline we now call Christianity. The influence of a person or group will dictate the actions of another person. It is your responsibility to choose who or what you will allow to have the power to influence your actions.

Negative peer pressure is one of the devices Satan uses to make young people choose unwise and unrighteous decisions. Peer pressure is good when there are positive outcomes to reach for. Peer pressure is not good when it causes you to do something that is wrong, something that is not comfortable, or something you do not want to do (going against your will). The company we surround ourselves with (environment), are the people we allow to influence us negatively or positively. For example, if you surround yourself with college-bound youth you have a higher likelihood of being in that category. On the other hand, if you surround yourself with youth who continually get into trouble, you have a higher likelihood of becoming like this category. As the old saying goes, "Birds of a feather, flock together."

The enemy's job is to make the sin look fun and living saved (Christ-like) look boring. Youth are driven by life, happiness, and energy. Therefore, the enemy attempts to move this image as far away from the church as possible. Have you ever wondered why there are not many Christian television shows on during "prime time" hours on "prime time" networks? Satan feels if he can influence you more with sin and worldliness, you are more likely to participate in sin! You should remember that what you surround yourself with will have the most power to influence you.

"Don't be fooled by those who say such thing, for bad company corrupts good character ~1 Corinthians 15:33."

Keeping the right influence

Remaining focused on where you are going with God will help you keep the wrong people or things from influencing you. It will also help guard you from allowing the effect of negative peer pressure to overtake your decisions in life. When you are focused on God's will and purpose, sin will not be able to have an upper hand. This is called walking in the spirit. Being led by

> *Does the company I keep help me or slow me down from making Godly decisions?*
>
> *What influences me to make the choices I make on a daily basis?*

God's spirit is the key to unmasking the deception of sin. Deception seeks to hide behind an emotion or feeling, but the Spirit of God reveals things according to the truth of God's word.

Being the influence

It is important to note that God made all His children with the power of influence. This characteristic He has given allows us to stand out from the world's way of what is considered normal.

This is why the enemy has to use deception—to change what is considered normal. The world considers lust and pride as normal, but God considers love and humility as normal (1 John 2:15, 1 Peter 5:6). The question raised is, "Is this spiritually normal or naturally normal?" Our stance with God makes us different from the world, but unified with the creator of our spiritual nature. This is why it is important to make the decision to be the influence of your environment, and not let your environment influence you.

You are created in the likeness of God. Being created in His likeness gives you the ability to transform generations. Every decision you make has an impact on another person. For example, you can choose to effect the lives of your peers to walk in a positive manner instead of a negative manner. Some will begin to walk a new path, due to your influence in their life. The strength you have to make the right choice in a difficult situation, can change the life of your peers for the better, leading them to have a desire to serve the God who gives you that strength.
"You are the light of the world---like a city on a mountain, glowing for all the world to see"
~Matthew 5:14.

Confession for life

- *I have been created by God for a purpose!*
- *My purpose is to give God glory by my lifestyle choices!*
- *I will not be persuaded by negative influences!*
- *God has given me the power to stand out from any negativity!*
- *I will show God's love through my lifestyle!*
- *I will continue to walk toward my destiny!*
- *I will not let sin have rule over my life, but I will walk humble before God, keeping myself pure at all times!*
- *Whatever career path I take, I will make sure I continue to bring God joy with my decisions!*
- *I will continue to walk toward my destiny, and ultimately walk in my destiny with God!*

~ In Jesus Name

You should make the decisions to be the influence of your environment and not let your environment influence you

3
Detours
Detour
Scriptures to help in times of need

Sexual Purity
1 Corinthians 3:16- Your body is the Temple of God
1 Corinthians 6:9-10- No fornicators in the Kingdom
1 Corinthians 6:19-20- Please God with your body
1 Corinthians 7:2- Marriage better than fornication

Depression
1 Thessalonians 5:17- Pray continually
Matthew 11:29- God gives rest
Psalms 18:6- God hears our distress

Lust
Romans 8:8- We cannot please God by our natural means
1 John 2:17- Lust passes away

Galatians 5:16- Walk in the Spirit

Peer Pressure
Exodus 23:1- Make no agreement with the wicked
Psalms 26:5- Do not sit with the wicked
Luke 11:26- Wicked spirits overtake a man

Anger
Ephesians 4:26- Be angry and do not sin
Galatians 5:22- Fruit of the spirit
Matthew 18:15- Solving disagreements

Alcohol
Galatians 5:21- Drunkenness will not inherit Kingdom
Proverbs 20:1- Wine is a mocker
Proverbs 23:21- Drunkard comes to poverty

Wild Partying
Galatians 5:21- Revellings (wild parties) will not inherit Kingdom
1 Peter 4:3- Revellings (wild parties) part of sin nature

Receiving Christ

Romans 10:9- For if you confess with your mouth that Jesus is Lord and believe in your heart that God raised him from the dead, you will be saved.

3 Steps to salvation
1. Recognize your need to be saved. Romans 3:23
2. Genuinely repent for sin. 2 Peter 3:9
3. Confess Jesus as Lord and Savior.

Father I come to you as a sinner. I repent for all the known and unknown sins I have done. I believe that Jesus died and rose again with all power, and I accept him as Lord of my life. I thank you now for being born again.

Now that you are saved continue to seek God's wisdom for your life and His word on how to conduct yourself as a Christian.

Pastor Lawrence Trimble is available to speak to your youth or congregation. If you would like to invite Lawrence Trimble to your event, youth group, church group, or organization you can contact him via email at
lawrencetrimble@gmail.com
telephone
217-519-6045, office

STRONG
PUBLISHING
House

Bringing the strength of your words to reality

For ordering information concerning this book or other
books, or if you would like information concerning publishing
you can contact us via email at
strongpublishinghouse@gmail.com
or visit our website at
strongpublishinghouse.weebly.com

Strong Publishing House
"Bringing the Strength of your words to reality"

www.ingramcontent.com/pod-product-compliance
Lightning Source LLC
Chambersburg PA
CBHW081238020426

42331CB00026B/3187